ABOUT CCLC

The Chesapeake Conservation Landscaping Council (CCLC) is a coalition of individuals
to researching, promoting, and educating the public about conservation-based lands
Chesapeake Bay Watershed. The Council is committed to implementing best practices that result in a healthier and
more beautiful environment benefiting residents and the region's biodiversity.

ABOUT THIS PUBLICATION

In late 2003, CCLC committee members began working on a set of materials to help define and guide conservation
landscaping practices. The intended audience ranges from professionals in the landscaping field to novice home
gardeners; from property managers at various types of facilities to local decision-makers. These written materials
have been through many revisions, with input from professionals with diverse backgrounds. Because of the nature
of the group (professionals volunteering their time), the subject matter (numerous choices of appropriate
practices), and the varied audience, development of a definitive, user-friendly format was challenging. Ultimately,
we intend to develop an interactive document for our website that shows examples of the Eight Elements,
especially as new technology and research evolves in the future. This document has been reviewed and refined by
our board members, and "put to the test" by entrants in our 2008 and 2010 landscape design contests. ***CCLC
welcomes feedback, recommendations, and new members willing and able to contribute their skills, knowledge,
and talents to future endeavors.*** Send comments to info@chesapeakelandscape.org

Other products of this CCLC committee have included development of the "Eight Elements of Conservation
Landscaping," a basic listing of the elements that will be more fully described in these guidelines; and a chapter on
conservation landscaping practices for the Maryland Nursery and Landscape Association's *Certified Professional
Horticulturists' Training Manual* (2005).

A number of other state and national efforts to define sustainable landscaping and/or lawn care practices have
occurred as CCLC members have developed these guidelines. Some are more focused and some more broadly
applicable. We recommend that practitioners review these materials for guidance as well. Though we will not
attempt to reference all of these other projects here, worth noting are the voluntary national guidelines and
performance benchmarks for sustainable land design, construction, and maintenance practices known as The
Sustainable Sites Initiative™, developed by the Lady Bird Johnson Wildflower Center (University of Texas at Austin),
the American Society of Landscape Architects, and the U.S. Botanic Garden. Learn more about The Sustainable
SITES Initiative™ at **www.sustainablesites.org**.

CCLC plans to publish this document as an online resource, and this goal is reflected in its design. Each chapter
contains basic information under a "HOW" section. The "LEARN MORE ABOUT IT" section provides additional
detail on words *highlighted* in the introductions and "HOW" section, which will appear in the online version of this
document as hyperlinks.

Contributing Authors 2003–2013
Britt Slattery, Maryland DNR (formerly U.S. Fish and Wildlife Service)
Rebecca Wertime, Alliance for the Chesapeake Bay
Carole Ann Barth, Heal Earth Gardens
Bob Campbell, National Park Service, Chesapeake Bay Program
Debbie Herr Cornwell, RLA, ASLA (formerly Herr Landscape Architecture and Environmental Design)
Meosotis Curtis, Montgomery County Department of Environmental Protection
Marcy Damon (formerly Chesapeake Bay Foundation)
Kathy Davis, (formerly University of Maryland Extension)
Suzanne Etgen, Arlington Echo Outdoor Education Center
Carol Jelich, University of Maryland Extension Master Gardener
Claudia Jones (formerly State of Maryland Chesapeake Bay Critical Area Commission)
Dr. Sylvan Kaufman, Sylvan Green Earth Consulting (formerly Adkins Arboretum)
Wanda MacLachlan, University of Maryland Extension
Dr. Sara Tangren, University of Maryland Extension (formerly Chesapeake Natives)

Cover photos courtesy of Ann Rohlfing, ARohlfing@aol.com. Book jacket design by Joanne Shipley.

TABLE OF CONTENTS

Introduction 1

The Eight Essential Elements of Conservation Landscaping. 2

Element 1. Design to Benefit the Environment 3

Element 2. Native Plants. 6

Element 3. Invasive Plant Management. 10

Element 4. Wildlife Habitat. 16

Element 5. Healthy Air Quality 20

Element 6. Clean Water 23

Element 7. Healthy Soils 28

Element 8. Management 33

TABLES AND ILLUSTRATIONS

List of Native Groundcovers 13

Short List of Common Invasive Plants 14

Figure 1. Evapotranspiration rates decrease and runoff increases as impervious surface increases 26

Formula to Calculate Amount of Mulch Needed 32

Seasonal Maintenance Calendar 37

INTRODUCTION

Why is Conservation Landscaping important in the Chesapeake Bay region?

People are a major cause of the Chesapeake Bay's problems. With so many people living and moving into the Bay watershed, nonpoint source pollution—that is, runoff from streets, farms, construction sites, and our own yards—has become an increasing problem. Contaminants from every home and community—sediments, sewage, manure, fertilizers, pesticides, herbicides, and motor oil—can be carried into the Bay from local streams and waterways.

Rising sea levels and the sinking of parts of the coastal plain threaten developed lands and natural areas in low-lying regions. Scientists predict that climate changes in our region will result in warmer winter temperatures and increased storm severity. These changes affect our plant choices as gardeners and how we manage our landscapes.

The Bay is part of a vast interconnected ecosystem, and everything we do on the land affects both local waters and the Bay. Because our actions are so closely linked to the health of the Chesapeake Bay, stewardship of the land and water in developed landscapes is our most effective tool for the Bay's restoration. How each of us manages property is important to us all. You can embrace the responsibility of caring for the land by following the principles of conservation landscaping at home and in your work.

The rewards of a well-maintained conservation landscape are many. It reflects positively on its owner and the professionals who were involved in design and installation. It beautifies the home and neighborhood—or the workplace, school, business, or park. It affords a comfortable place to entertain, relax, play, work, and learn. Most importantly, it provides and promotes a safer and healthier environment for our use and enjoyment, allowing us to live in harmony with local natural resources.

Engaging in the conservation landscaping practices described here can make an important difference in helping preserve the region's plants, habitats, and animals, all critical elements in the complex web of life that characterizes the Chesapeake Bay and its surrounding watershed.

What is Conservation Landscaping?

Working with nature to reduce pollution, conservation landscaping incorporates environmentally sensitive design, low impact development, non-invasive native and beneficial plants, and integrated pest management to create diverse landscapes that help protect clean air and water, support wildlife, and provide a healthier and more beautiful human environment.

Conservation landscaping supports clean air and water by:
- Using plants that are adapted to local conditions and thus require less fertilizer and pesticides
- Trapping localized stormwater on site with rain barrels and rain gardens to ensure slow percolation and increased filtration of nutrients entering the groundwater
- Reducing the amount of smog released into the air and the amount of atmospheric deposition of nutrients into our water by reducing the amount of mowable lawn area

Conservation landscaping supports wildlife by:
- Providing a diverse plant environment that attracts greater animal diversity and fosters healthier ecological communities
- Creating migratory corridors of conjoined healthy ecological communities

Conservation landscaping supports a healthier and more beautiful human environment by:
- Reducing the amount of pollution entering the environment
- Demonstrating the beauty of well-maintained, natural landscaping

THE EIGHT ESSENTIAL ELEMENTS
of Conservation Landscaping

The following elements represent the practice of conservation landscaping. By implementing these practices, you can contribute to the restoration of the *Chesapeake Bay watershed** and improve the region's water and air quality. Incorporate as many of these elements as possible into your landscape, to benefit all life in our watershed.

A conservation landscape:

1. Is designed to benefit the environment and function efficiently and aesthetically for human use and well-being;

2. Uses locally native plants that are appropriate for site conditions;

3. Institutes a management plan for the removal of existing invasive plants and the prevention of future nonnative plant invasions;

4. Provides habitat for wildlife;

5. Promotes healthy air quality and minimizes air pollution;

6. Conserves and cleans water;

7. Promotes healthy soils;

8. Is managed to conserve energy, reduce waste, and eliminate or minimize the use of pesticides and fertilizers.

Chesapeake Bay watershed*—see a map at **pubs.usgs.gov/fs/fs12497/fig1.html

1   DESIGN TO BENEFIT THE ENVIRONMENT

A conservation landscape is designed to benefit the environment and function efficiently and aesthetically for human use and well-being.

Conservation landscape design occurs in the context of nature. It seeks to preserve, enhance, and reduce impacts upon a site's natural features. Landscape design is the initial investment that allows you to make the most of the site you have without expending resources to drastically alter the site.

HOW

To design a conservation landscape:

- Perform a site analysis. Consider the character of the site (or regional attributes), historic uses of the land, soil types, geology, sun, water, natural plant communities, and the environmental features on adjacent properties. Environmental features describe a combination of conditions such as a sunny slope, or a marshy low area.

- Choose your *goals* for the landscape. Consider any specific *needs* that are related to those goals. Then plan a landscape that considers Essential Elements 2 through 6 while achieving your goals and meeting your needs.

- Pay attention to phases. For example, don't put in the landscape before the utility lines are installed. Your landscape design may be *simple or involved* or somewhere in between. If your project is complex, it is especially important to pay attention to the separate phases of the project and their sequencing.

- Think of landscape design as an ongoing process. Update your design and your maintenance plan according to the conditions of the landscape and the needs of the people using it. In many cases, landscape designs will need to be edited annually.

- Preserve *existing environmental features* to the greatest possible degree.

- Restore degraded environmental features where opportunities exist. For example, institute an invasive species management plan for an onsite woodland, add to the species diversity of a degraded wetland, or build links between existing isolated habitats.

- Take advantage of opportunities to create *new environmental features*. For example, transition into adjacent natural areas to expand their size or put in a feature that creates a new habitat such as a small pond. Link adjacent natural areas or transition into them.

- Address the landscape implications of Essential Elements 2 through 8 during the design phase. For example, you could add a pond to the design to create wildlife habitat (Element 4). To improve water quality (Element 6), you could design to reduce impervious surfaces. Or, to promote healthy soil (Element 7), you could design in a compost facility. More information on each Element is found in sections 2 through 8.

- Keep lawn to the minimum area needed for function. Conventional lawns are composed of alien invasive plants, such as tall fescue, that have high maintenance requirements in terms of water input, fertilization, and herbicide use. However, because they provide a smooth surface for certain recreational activities, a poor habitat for ticks and other pests of concern, and because the look of lawn is so strongly expected from some members of the community, even conservation landscapes often need to contain some lawn to be functional. Also consider the extent to which any conventional lawn that must be present can be maintained with minimized input without compromising function.

- Mirror patterns found in nature. For example, naturalistic layering of trees, shrubs, and herbaceous plants provides structure that is both important to wildlife and attractive to people.

LEARN MORE ABOUT IT

GOALS AND NEEDS IN LANDSCAPE DESIGN

Choose your goals for the landscape. Consider any specific needs that are related to those goals. Then plan a landscape that considers Essential Elements 2 through 8 while achieving your goals and meeting your needs.

GOALS

Start by determining your goals for the landscape. Your goals may contain multiple environmental benefits as well as benefits that are not specifically related to the environment but that can be accomplished in an environmentally sound way. Some common examples of landscape goals include:
- Screening an unsightly view;
- Creating pollinator habitat in the home landscape;
- Creating a lovely and functional corporate landscape;
- Striving for low maintenance;
- Providing a safe environment for children;
- Adding more color and interest in a schoolyard setting;
- Capturing and treating runoff from the site and from adjacent properties.

NEEDS

Plan your landscape with your goals in mind, and then consider what you will need in order to achieve your goals. For example:

- To screen an unsightly view, you will need a fence with an evergreen vine, or a row of evergreen shrubs or trees.

- To provide pollinator habitat, choose native plants, including host and nectar plants, a water source, and shelter.

- To create a lovely and functional corporate landscape, you may still need a parking lot of a certain size and/or type of loading docks. If so, how will you minimize impervious surfaces while maximizing function? Will you need the landscape to be colorful and interesting in all four seasons? Would outdoor trails, rain gardens, and/or picnic tables help you meet your goals?

- For a low maintenance landscape, install large islands of shrub and tree plantings. How will you keep mowing, and especially mowing around obstacles, to a minimum?

- To create a safe environment for children, your landscape should be free of potential poisons like fertilizers, herbicides, fungicides and insecticides. Do you know how to recognize poisonous plants and be equipped to eliminate them from the landscape?

- To provide color and interest for a school landscape, consider a landscape plan that focuses on spring and fall color when school is in session. Do you also need landscape elements that provide educational benefits, such as rain gardens, water gardens, and pollinator gardens? Do you need interpretive signs?

SIMPLE AND INVOLVED LANDSCAPE DESIGNS

Pay attention to phases. Your landscape design may be simple or involved or somewhere in between. If your project is complex, it will be especially important to pay attention to the separate phases of the project and their sequencing.

Do you have a small, simple landscape project or a large, complicated one? A homeowner designing the landscape for a row house has an easier job than the developer of a new commercial project. If your project is small, you may have a hard time fitting in enough species of plants to provide year-round color and interest. If your project is involved, it will be especially important to pay attention to the separate phases of the project and their timing. For example, you will want to make sure all septic or utility lines are dug before the landscaping is installed.

ENVIRONMENTAL LANDSCAPE FEATURES: EXISTING AND NEW

Preserve *existing environmental features* to the greatest possible degree. Take advantage of opportunities to create *new environmental features* where none existed before.

In designing a landscape, consider existing landscape features (for example, forests, individual trees that are large or especially ecologically or aesthetically valuable, highly erodible soils, an eagle's nest, high water tables, waterways and wetlands, meadows, animal communities, areas of undisturbed native soils, rock formations) that can be preserved and folded into the new plan for the landscape.

Some landscapes present opportunities to create new environmental components. Examples include planting forests where none have existed for a long time, converting a lawn to a meadow, or constructing a wetland at a closed mine. However, destroying a healthy landscape feature to create another type of feature (for instance, cutting down a mature forest to create a pond) is obviously counter to the intentions of conservation landscaping.

REFERENCES AND RESOURCES

- The Sustainable SITES Initiative™: **www.sustainablesites.org/**
- Landscape for Life: **www.landscapeforlife.org/**
- Beck, Travis. 2013. *Principles of Ecological Landscape Design*. Island Press, Washington, DC.

2 NATIVE PLANTS

A conservation landscape uses locally native plants that are appropriate for site conditions.

Native plants are those that are naturally present in this <u>region</u> since the last ice age.* Since records of native plants were not written until the seventeenth and eighteenth centuries, most native plant lists refer back to this time. Alien or introduced plants are those that have been brought to the region as a consequence of human action. In conservation landscapes, <u>cultivars</u> (cultivated varieties) of native plants do not deliver the same benefits as the true species of locally native plants and are not considered native plants in this discussion.

Balanced communities of native plants contribute to the biodiversity of the landscape. Native plants have <u>co-evolved</u> with associated animals to form interdependent communities. Properly sited native plants are adapted to local conditions. Consequently, once established, they require little extra water, fertilizer, or pesticides. Native plants express the character of our natural landscape in a way that alien plants cannot.

Climate change has resulted in a shift in hardiness zones, making it important to learn about the natural ranges of plants. If a plant in your area is growing at the southern limit of its range, it will be harder to continue to grow that plant in future. It is important to preserve the genetic variability of native plants to ensure that some can adapt to climate change. Selecting locally native plants over cultivars can help expand local populations and give them a better chance of surviving and reproducing.

***Note:** Definitions of native plants vary slightly among groups. CCLC chooses this easy definition for the purposes of this document. The Federal Native Plant Conservation Committee (1994) defines a native as a plant species "that occurs naturally in a particular region, state, ecosystem, and habitat without direct or indirect human actions."*

HOW

A conservation landscape contains locally native plants that are appropriate for site conditions:

- See resources listed below to determine which plants are <u>native</u> to your site.
- Choose the right plant for the right place. Select plants suited to existing soil, moisture, sunlight, and other site conditions.
- When selecting a long-lived plant, consider how that plant is likely to grow as the climate shifts to warmer winters and more extreme periods of drought and flooding.
- Native plants may occasionally be obtained from the wild, as with plant rescues or wild seed collection. In general, however, native plants should not be taken directly from the wild.
- To find commercial sources of native plants, see resources listed below. Always ask nurseries about the source of the native species sold.
- Include a diversity of native plants to provide a wide variety of benefits.
- Pick native plants that complement nearby natural areas by using similar species composition. For example, when planting adjacent to an oak-hickory forest, consider selecting species from that natural community.

LEARN MORE ABOUT IT

REGION

Region is defined as within about a 200-mile radius of, and in the same physiographic province (Coastal Plain, Piedmont, Mountain) as, the site to be planted.

CULTIVARS

Cultivated varieties (*cultivars*) are available for many native plants. These plants have been nursery grown as "improved" selections to provide plants with certain physical characteristics, such as a different flower color, a particular foliage shape, early bloom time, or compact size. All the plants belonging to a particular cultivar are genetically identical.

Although gardening with cultivars may be suitable to meet aesthetic goals, those planning habitat projects to provide food and cover for wildlife should use as many true species (not cultivars) as possible. No one really knows how these cultivars will affect the wildlife that depends on local native plant species for food. If a local native plant's bloom period, color, fragrance, or flower shape is changed, it could have a serious detrimental effect on the hummingbirds, bees, butterflies, and other wildlife that may use that plant. True species are most suited for use by native wildlife, and planting them will increase your chances of attracting these creatures.

In addition, research has shown that some cultivars breed with local native plants and thus decrease a population's fitness or ability to survive in an area. If the planting site is near designated natural areas, it is best to avoid using cultivars so that these genetically homogenous plants don't end up cross-breeding with native species and "contaminating" or changing the natural gene pool. Since cultivars often lack the genetic diversity necessary to adapt to local environmental conditions, they may not thrive, and cross-breeding could lead to eventual extinction of existing natives. Since we can't know the full extent of how this would affect local native plant populations and all life that is interdependent with them, we must work to protect natural biodiversity. Cultivars of locally rare species may be available in the nursery trade but should not be used for landscaping—check state and Federal lists of rare, threatened, and endangered species at **www.fws.gov/endangered**.

CO-EVOLUTION AND INTERDEPENDENCE

Charles Darwin's work contributes much to our understanding of evolution. There are specific relationships: an insect that specializes in feeding on nectar from deep flowers is dependent upon a deep-flowered plant. The plant, in turn, is specialized for being pollinated by insects with long mouthparts. We don't know all of these relationships, but we understand that countless numbers exist and that they are critical to sustaining life as we know it. Organisms both cooperate and compete in ecosystems. The interrelationships and interdependencies of these organisms are related to the long-term stability of populations and ecosystems—what allows Earth to be self-sustaining.

In order to reproduce, many plants depend upon insects or other creatures for pollination and seed dispersal. Some of these animals have evolved to use specific plants as sources of food (usually nectar or pollen). The exchange of genetic material through pollination (sexual reproduction) allows ensuing generations of plants to adapt to environmental conditions and survive through natural selection. The great diversity of organisms is the result of more than 3.5 billion years of evolution that has filled the world with life forms.

There are 100,000 kinds of insects and 1,200 birds and mammals that are involved in pollinating both wild plants and our cultivated crops worldwide. Wild pollinators are responsible for about one third of the food that humans eat. Habitat loss and fragmentation, and use of chemical pesticides, are major causes of reduced pollinator populations.

See more on co-evolution at **www.ditext.com/ehrlich/appendix.html**.
See also: *The flower and the fly: long insect mouthparts and deep floral tubes...*, ***Natural History*, March, 2005** by **Laura A. Session** and **Steven D. Johnson**.

Plants labeled as "native" or "wildflower" are not necessarily native to our region. It is important to refer to an independent reference for the local region in which the plants will be planted. Check with your state's Natural Heritage office, consult regional flora, or find resources through a local native plant society.

Even though a plant seems to occur naturally or "grow wild" in your yard or in the wild, this does not mean that the plant is native. Many alien plants "grow wild," and these are called "naturalized" or, in extreme cases, invasive. This means that these plants have the ability to spread and thrive outside of their cultivated location, potentially threatening the integrity of nearby natural areas.

Native Plant Nurseries
- Native plant nurseries in Maryland: **www.mdflora.org/publications/nurseries.html**
- Native plant nurseries in Virginia: **vnps.org/wp/vnps-native-plant-nurseries-and-plant-sales/**
- Native plant nurseries in the Chesapeake Bay region: **www.fws.gov/chesapeakebay/bayscapes/bsresources/bs-nurseries.html**

REFERENCES AND RESOURCES

- Slattery, Britt E., Kathryn Reshetiloff, and Susan M. Zwicker. *Native Plants for Wildlife Habitat and Conservation Landscaping: Chesapeake Bay Watershed.* U.S. Fish & Wildlife Service, Chesapeake Bay Field Office, 2005. **www.nps.gov/plants/pubs/chesapeake/index.htm**
- Delaware Native Plant Society (DNPS): **www.delawarenativeplants.org**
- Maryland Native Plant Society (MNPS): **www.mdflora.org**
- Virginia Native Plant Society (VNPS): **www.vnps.org**
- Pennsylvania Native Plant Society: **www.pawildflower.org**
- West Virginia Native Plant Society www.wvnps.org
- Lady Bird Johnson Wildflower Center's Native Plant Bibliography: **www.wildflower.org/bibliography/**
- Plant Conservation Alliance: **www.nps.gov/plants**
- PLANTS National Database, U.S. Department of Agriculture Natural Resource Conservation Service: **plants.usda.gov**
- Flora of Delaware, Delaware Department of Natural Resources and Environmental Control, 2001. **www.dnrec.state.de.us/fw/floraform.pdf**
- *The Plants of Pennsylvania: An Illustrated Manual*, Ann Fowler Rhoads, Timothy A. Block, 2nd ed. 2007. **www.upenn.edu/pennpress/book/14335.html**
- Landscaping with Native Plants in Pennsylvania: **www.dcnr.state.pa.us/forestry/wildplant/native.aspx**
- Flora of North America: **hua.huh.harvard.edu/FNA/**
- Flora of Virginia: **www.floraofvirginia.org**
- Flora of Virginia online: **www.vaplantatlas.org**
- Flora of the Washington-Baltimore Area, Smithsonian Institution: **persoon.si.edu/DCflora/**
- Integrated Taxonomic Information System (authority on current Latin names for plants and animals): **www.itis.gov/**
- U.S. Department of Agriculture Forest Service Silvics Manual (tree identification, info, etc.): **www.na.fs.fed.us/spfo/pubs/silvics_manual/table_of_contents.htm**
- Virginia Tech's Dendrology website for identifying woody plants: **www.cnr.vt.edu/dendro/dendrology/idit.htm**
- The Alliance for Chesapeake Bay: **www.allianceforthebay.org**
- BayScapes Program, U.S. Fish and Wildlife Service, including links to references, nurseries, and more: **www.fws.gov/ChesapeakeBay/Bayscapes.htm**
- Audubon at Home, National Audubon Society and Audubon Maryland-DC: **www.audubonathome.org** and **www.audubonmddc.org**
- Maryland Bay-Wise Program: **www.extension.umd.edu/baywise**

- Chesapeake Conservation Landscaping Council: **www.ChesapeakeLandscape.org**
- Ecological Landscaping Association: **www.ecolandscaping.org**
- Environmental Protection Agency's Green Landscaping with Native Plants: **www.epa.gov/greenacres**
- Maryland Home and Garden Information Center (MD Cooperative Extension): **www.extension.umd.edu/hgic**
- Missouri Botanic Gardens Plantfinder: **www.mobot.org**
- Native Plants for Conservation, Restoration & Landscaping (including grassland plants; set of brochures): **www.dcr.virginia.gov/natural_heritage/nativeplants.shtml**
- Native Plants Network (propagation information): **www.nativeplantnetwork.org/network**
- National Wildlife Federation's Backyard Habitats Program: **www.nwf.org/backyard**
- The Wild Ones (organization of natural landscapers): **www.for-wild.org**
- Hightshoe, Gary L. *Native Trees, Shrubs, and Vines for Urban and Rural America: A Planting Design Manual for Environmental Designers*. 1987, John Wiley & Sons.
- Leopold, Donald J. *Native Plants of the Northeast: a Guide for Gardening and Conservation*. 2005, Timber Press.

3 INVASIVE PLANT MANAGEMENT

A conservation landscape institutes a management plan for the removal of existing invasive plants and the prevention of future nonnative plant invasions.

Alien plants are those that occur artificially in locations beyond their known historical natural ranges, most often brought to new regions by humans through horticultural or accidental introductions. *Invasive plants* are those aliens that display rapid growth and spread, allowing them to establish over large areas. Outside of their natural native range, these plants encounter fewer of the conditions, competitors, or pests that keep them in check back "at home." Their phenomenal growth allows them to overwhelm and displace existing vegetation and form dense one-species stands. Wind, water flow, birds and other wildlife, movement of soil, and other factors can spread invasive plants to natural areas, causing significant ecological harm. Invasive plants can alter fire frequencies, soil chemistry, and erosion rates. They can degrade or change wildlife habitat, food quality, and availability. They can displace native plants through competition for water, nutrients, light, or space for establishment, reducing natives' establishment, growth, or reproduction. They can alter native populations through hybridization. For more information on invasive plants, see the recommendations in the references section of this chapter. A _weed_ is any plant, native or alien, that is out of place, growing where it is not wanted in the landscape.

HOW

- First, do no harm.
- Before adding a new plant to your landscape, check to ensure that it is:
  - *Native* (see resources in Element 2, Native Plants) or
  - If alien, then **not** *invasive* (see authoritative resources on invasive plants below)
- Remove existing invasive plants.

  - Be suspicious of plants that are acting like thugs in the landscape. Plants that spread quickly, engulf other plants, dominate the landscape, or produce large seed heads or copious berries may be problematic. Identification is necessary. If the plant is alien, it needs to be eradicated. If native, the landscape manager needs to decide whether this _aggressive native plant_ is desirable.

  - Many old familiar landscape favorites may be invasive and should be evaluated. Unfortunately, many *commonly used landscaping plants are invasive*. A few examples are English ivy, common orange daylily, Japanese pachysandra, Bradford or Callery pear, burning bush, Japanese barberry, Miscanthus, and Liriope.

  - A plant may be invasive even though it never spreads within your garden. Pollen and/or seeds can be carried from your site by wind, water, and wildlife and take hold in suitable natural habitats.

  - Unwanted or alien plants that appear in a planting bed and choke or outcompete what was planted, or detract from desired aesthetics, will need to be removed. Invasive alien species, state-designated noxious weeds, and even aggressive native plants require control. Each situation requires identification and analysis of the vegetation. Fortunately, many resources are available to help.

    - Consult the printed publications and websites listed below for plant-specific information. Be aware that many documents are not all inclusive, and their authors may not have intended them to be.

    - *Free expert help* in identifying plant material is available from your local university cooperative extension office.

- English ivy, periwinkle, creeping lily turf (*Liriope*), and Japanese pachysandra are some commonly used groundcovers, particularly for shade. However, these species are aliens that are invasive in the

  landscape. They should be avoided, and native alternatives selected instead. A groundcover can be any plant that physically covers or hides the bare ground from view; it does not have to be evergreen, or a single species. From a conservation landscaping perspective, any herbaceous or low-growing woody native plant is a good groundcover. A number of *native selections* will perform well where a low-growing, creeping, spreading, or clump-forming plant is most desired.

- When disturbing an area, take steps to prevent invasion of opportunistic alien plants by planting desirable native vegetation. For example, in a new development, you can "armor the edge" by planting natives along the limit of disturbance. Or, if removing existing vegetation in a yard, think about what you want to occupy the space next.

- *Management* is an ongoing process. Over time, the following steps must recur on a regular basis:
  - Identify invasive plant problems
  - Prioritize plant problems
  - Implement removal according to priorities
  - Edit your landscape plantings, adding native plants where needed to fill gaps
  - Scout for missed problem plants and new infestations
  - Keep abreast of current information on invasive species and their control

LEARN MORE ABOUT IT

AGGRESSIVE NATIVE PLANTS

Why are certain native plants "aggressive" and alien plants "invasive"? Those alien or non-native plants that are deemed "invasive" are species that come from elsewhere, escape cultivation, and colonize rapidly. These plants can take over an entire natural area in a relatively short period of time: a woodland floor covered by a sea of garlic mustard; a forest buried under kudzu, oriental bittersweet, or Japanese honeysuckle; a wetland overtaken by purple loosestrife. In contrast, although some native species can spread well beyond their intended boundaries, they are prone to more limitations across the landscape—soil conditions, light, etc.—than invasive aliens, and so most "aggressive" natives do not have sweepingly destructive capabilities. Though black-eyed Susans may seed themselves throughout a garden, they will eventually give way to other species and will not encroach upon the entire surrounding neighborhood. There are a few native "thugs" that can present quite a challenge in managing larger properties—poison ivy, greenbrier, and cattails, for instance—but they do provide wildlife benefits. Although these need some control to uphold a diverse landscape, they are a piece in the biodiversity puzzle and therefore they do not need to be eradicated.

Some native species demonstrate aggressive behavior and rapid spread. While these should be planted cautiously in your garden, they do not usually pose a threat to natural areas, habitats, or native plant populations. Because they are native, they normally have some natural controls or limitations (site conditions, predators or pests, competition with other species, etc.). In some circumstances, such as planting for soil stabilization or groundcover, rapid spread can be a desirable attribute. A few native plants that should be planted carefully in the garden and watched for spread include black-eyed Susans (*Rudbeckia* species), mint family plants such as bee balm (*Monarda* species) and false dragonhead (*Physostegia virginiana*), switchgrass (*Panicum virgatum*), river oats (*Chasmanthium latifolium*), asters (*Aster or Symphiotrichum novae-angliae* or *novi-belgii*), eastern columbine (*Aquilegia canadensis*), golden groundsel (*Senecio or Packera aureus*), and trumpet creeper (*Campsis radicans*).

WEEDS

Some desirable plants, such as butterfly milkweed (*Asclepias tuberosa*), have the word "weed" in their names. This simply refers to "wort," an early English word for an herbaceous plant. The term "weed" is also used for a plant that is out of place. A weed could be a native or non-native aggressively growing plant. Sometimes a plant can be a weed in one situation and a desirable plant in another situation. Most states have a *noxious weeds* law that requires landowners to control certain plants. Generally, noxious weed laws govern weeds of agricultural and grazing lands.

MANAGEMENT

Numerous options exist for managing invasive plants. The categories of management are biological control, manual and mechanical control, and chemical control. Biological control most commonly employs grazing animals such as goats and sheep, as well as introduced host-specific insects, to control invasive plants. Manual and mechanical control includes hand-pulling, cutting, mowing, and burning. Chemical control uses herbicides to kill plants. Each technique has its benefits and drawbacks, and the technique you choose should depend on the types of plants you are controlling, the site you are working on, your budget, and how much time you have. Remember that the sooner you detect a small population of an invasive plant, the easier it will be to control it! The references below contain additional information on control techniques. Any management of invasive plants should take into consideration the other plants and animals that use the site and how the site will be restored after the invasive plants are removed.

FREE EXPERT HELP

- Digital photos of plants may be e-mailed to the Home and Garden Information Center, **www.extension.umd.edu/hgic.**
- The Maryland Native Plant Society (**www.mdflora.org)** holds plant identification clinics a half hour before monthly meetings.

Instead of the "usual" invasive species used as groundcovers (English ivy, pachysandra, etc.), choose natives that accomplish the same effect safely. There are many, many options, but a few good choices to start with include the following:

Herbaceous, flowering
Aquilegia canadensis, eastern or wild columbine
Asarum canadense, wild ginger
Chrysogonum virginianum, green-and-gold
Chrysopsis mariana, Maryland golden aster
Coreopsis verticillata, threadleaf coreopsis
Geranium maculatum, wild geranium
Heuchera americana,H. villosa, alumroot, hairy heuchera
Mitchella repens, partridgeberry
Phlox carolina, P. divaricata, P. maculata, P. paniculata, P. stolonifera, P. subulata, phloxes (thick-leaved, woodland or wild blue, meadow, summer, creeping, moss)
Senecio aureus (Packera aurea), golden ragwort, golden groundsel
Tiarella cordifolia, foamflower

Ferns
Dryopteris cristata, D. intermedia, D. marginalis, crested woodfern, evergreen woodfern, marginal shield fern
Osmunda cinnamomea, cinnamon fern

Grasses
Carex glaucodea, C. pensylvanica, blue wood sedge, Pennsylvania sedge
Danthonia spicata, poverty oatgrass

Shrubs
Gaultheria procumbens, wintergreen, checkerberry
Vaccinium angustifolium, lowbush blueberry

EXAMPLES OF COMMONLY USED INVASIVE LANDSCAPING PLANTS

The following list includes just some of the numerous exotic species that are commonly used for landscaping. This practice should be discontinued because these species spread into the landscape and threaten our valuable natural areas. Some plants included here may not be commonly planted but are found frequently, even in suburban yards, so the professional should be able to recognize them. *Avoid planting any of these species, and urge property owners to control or eradicate them where they exist.* Information on their biology, control, and native alternatives can be found in the references listed with this chapter.

Trees
Acer ginnala, amur maple
Acer platanoides, Norway maple
Ailanthus altissima, tree of heaven
Albizia julibrissin, silk tree, mimosa tree
Broussonetia papyrifera, paper mulberry
Morus alba, white mulberry
Paulownia tomentosa, princess tree
Pyrus calleryana, Bradford or Callery pear
Quercus acutissima, sawtooth oak

Shrubs
Berberis thunbergii, Japanese barberry
Buddleia davidii, other species, butterfly bush
Elaeagnus umbellata, autumn olive
Euonymus alatus, winged burning bush
Ligustrum species, privets (several species)
Lonicera tatarica, L. maackii, L. morrowii, bush honeysuckles
Nandina domestica, heavenly bamboo
Rhamnus cathartica, buckthorn
Rhodotypos scandens, jetbead
Rosa multiflora, multiflora rose
Rubus phoenicolasius, wineberry
Spiraea japonica, Japanese spiraea, Japanese meadowsweet
Viburnum dilatatum , V. lantana ,V. opulus, V. plicatum, V. sieboldii, non-native viburnums

Vines
Akebia quinata, five-leaved akebia
Ampelopsis brevipedunculata, porcelainberry
Celastrus orbiculatus, oriental bittersweet
Cynanchum louiseae, Louis' swallowwort
Euonymus fortunei, creeping euonymus, winter creeper
Hedera helix, English ivy
Lonicera japonica, Japanese honeysuckle
Polygonum perfoliatum, mile-a-minute
Pueraria montana v. lobata, kudzu
Vinca minor, periwinkle
Wisteria sinensis, W. floribunda, Chinese and Japanese wisteria

Herbaceous Plants
Arundo donax, giant reed, wild cane
Bambusa, Phyllostachys, Pseudosasa spp., running bamboos
Bromus sterilis and other species, poverty brome grass
Coronilla varia, crown vetch
Hemerocallis fulva, H. lilioasphodelus, common daylily, yellow daylily
Hesperis matronalis, dame's rocket
Iris pseudacorus, yellow iris
Lespedeza cuneata, Chinese lespedeza
Leucanthemum vulgare, ox-eye daisy
Liriope spicatum, Liriope, creeping lily turf
Lythrum salicaria (all cultivars), purple loosestrife
Miscanthus sinensis, Chinese silver grass, maiden hair
Pachysandra terminalis, Japanese pachysandra
Perilla frutescens, beefsteak plant
Phragmites australis, common reed
Polygonum cuspidatum , Japanese knotweed
Ranunculus ficaria, lesser celandine

Aquatic Plants
Eichhornia crassipes, water hyacinth
Hydrilla verticillata, hydrilla
Myriophyllum aquaticum, parrot feather watermilfoil
Myriophyllum spicatum, Eurasian watermilfoil
Salvinia molesta, giant salvinia
Trapa natans, water chestnut

WEBSITES AND REFERENCES

- Center for Invasive Plant Management: **www.weedcenter.org/management/control.html**
- Maryland Invasive Species Council: **www.mdinvasivesp.org**
- Mid-Atlantic Invasive Plant Council: **www.maipc.org**
- National Invasive Species Council: **www.invasivespecies.gov**
- TNC's Bad Plants In Your Backyard initiative: **www.nature.org/ourinitiatives/habitats/forests/explore/backyard-invasives.xml**
- Plant Conservation Alliance, Alien Plants Working Group, "Weeds Gone Wild," factsheets on many invasive species: **www.nps.gov/plants/alien**
- Univ. of Georgia, Bugwood Network, Invasive and Exotic Species of North America: **www.invasive.org**
- U.S. Fish and Wildlife Service, BayScapes Program: **www.fws.gov/chesapeakebay/bayscapes.htm**; **chesapeakebay.fws.gov**
- *Plant Invaders of Mid-Atlantic Natural Areas* (U.S. Fish and Wildlife Service and National Park Service guide to ID and control of 48 invasives; also includes native plant alternatives to some common invasive landscaping plants): **www.nps.gov/plants/alien/pubs/midatlantic**
- *Nonnative Invasive Plants of Southern Forests*, USDA Forest Service: **www.invasive.org/eastern/srs**
- *Southeast Exotic Pest Plant Council Invasive Plant Manual*: **www.invasive.org/eastern/eppc**
- Kaufman, Sylvan R. and Wallace Kaufman. *Invasive Plants: Guide to Identification and the Impacts and Control of Common North American Species.* Stackpole Books, 2013.
- Maryland Department of Natural Resources: information, species list, etc. at **www.dnr.state.md.us/invasives/** and a citizen's guide to wetland invasives at **www.dnr.state.md.us/forests/pdfs/ACB_ControlofInvasivePlants.pdf**
- Uva, R.H., J.C. Neal, J.M. DiTomaso. *Weeds of the Northeast.* Cornell University Press, 1997.
- State noxious weed lists: These are the plants for which states *require* control measures. Most are focused on threats to agricultural lands, not natural areas, and therefore do not include all plants considered invasive in a state. For information on state noxious weed laws and invasive species plant lists, start with **www.invasive.org/maps/states.cfm**

4 WILDLIFE HABITAT

A conservation landscape provides habitat for wildlife.

One of the most important and rewarding aspects of conservation landscaping is providing for *native wildlife species* such as birds, butterflies, bees, spiders, fish, frogs, salamanders, snakes, and other animals. An animal's *habitat* is the particular type of area where it finds food, water, shelter, and breeding or nesting space. Biodiversity—a wide variety of native plant and animal life—is critical to maintaining a healthy *ecosystem*. For many reasons, the amount and quality of habitat for wildlife is declining across the landscape. First and foremost, plan your landscape to conserve and protect existing wildlife habitat. Larger-scale habitat protection and restoration are most critical to conserving wildlife populations. While simply planting native plants is not the complete answer, practicing conservation landscaping does contribute to overall restoration of the local environment. Creating conservation landscapes in residential yards, neighborhoods, and parks, and on business, school, and municipal properties, will help to increase available habitat for wildlife.

In order to have the greatest ecological value for wildlife, conservation landscapes need to mimic natural plant groupings and incorporate features that provide as many habitat elements as possible. Develop landscaping that complements and links to existing natural areas. Providing a diversity of food sources and places for shelter or nesting, as well as sources of water, will help support a variety of enjoyable, beneficial wildlife.

HOW

To improve the planned landscape so that it supports a diversity of wildlife species, we must minimize lawn and improve vegetative structure (landscape with layers of plants), similar to what nature provides in wetlands, meadows, and forests. A conservation landscape can attract native wildlife based on wise choices and planning that will benefit the local environment as well as the homeowner. Conservation landscaping can be used to create corridors and transition zones for wildlife in a landscape otherwise fragmented by housing and shopping areas, roads, office buildings, and other development.

As conservation landscaping is planned, consider the following to benefit wildlife:

- Provide *food* sources year-round. The leaves, stems, twigs, bark, flowers (nectar), seeds, and fruits (e.g., nuts, berries) of native plants form the basis of many animals' food needs. The food web is very complex. Some animals eat plants, others eat insects or other animals, and some eat both. Providing the plants helps attract and provide various components of the web, thus supporting a diversity of species. [See Element 2, Native Plants}.

- Include a *water source*. Water is important to all living creatures, including insects, and is needed year-round for survival. Include water in landscape plans to benefit wildlife—whether a small bird bath, a small lined pond, a large pond with a wetland edge, or anything in between.

- Provide *structure*. Use layers of plant types, heights, and arrangements that mirror nature to provide needed shelter from the elements and nesting space important to many types of wildlife. [See Element 2, Native Plants].

- Supply *cover*. Brush piles, rock outcrops or walls, and hedgerows are features to consider including if the site is appropriate, as these provide protection from predators and other threats.

Consider using alternatives to pesticides. All life, including humans and pets, is susceptible to harm from pesticide use. Spraying to rid the yard of an insect pest can also kill butterflies and their larvae, birds eating affected insects can become ill, and the effects are magnified up the food chain. Instead, choose safer options (the least toxic but still effective method). [See *Manage Garden Pests with Integrated Pest Management (IPM)* in Element 8, Management.]

LEARN MORE ABOUT IT

HABITAT

Habitat types include various kinds of wetlands, forests, meadows, and aquatic areas such as streams, rivers, ponds, and estuaries. Environmental degradation and direct destruction are just two factors leading to wildlife habitat decline. Increasing development accelerates habitat loss, replacing natural areas and creating an abundance of lawn and pavement that in turn shed more rainwater and further contribute to water pollution and habitat degradation. Development fragments habitats, making it more difficult for species to migrate seasonally or to move in response to climate change.

NATIVE ANIMAL SPECIES

The value of native wildlife cannot be overstated. The history of the Chesapeake Bay region is inextricably linked to the value of its natural resources. The abundance of wildlife supported by the habitats and landscapes within its vast watershed enriches our way of life and our economy in many ways—from the seafood industry, to tourism, to local recreation. The Bay region supports 3,600 species of plant and animal life, including more than 300 fish species and 2,700 plant types. Bird watching, wildlife viewing, and nature photography are currently the fastest-growing nature-related recreation activities. Regardless of whether nature is the primary focus of people's activities, in periodic opinion surveys respondents place high importance and intrinsic value on the presence of a diversity of plants and animals. *Pollinators* such as bees, moths, butterflies, bats, and hummingbirds are critical to the continued survival of both native plant populations and our cultivated food crops. [See *Cultivars* in Element 2, Native Plants.] Protecting, conserving, and restoring our natural resources is critical in maintaining quality of life, now and for future generations.

Plants are one of the most important features of an animal's habitat because they often provide most, if not all, of the animal's habitat needs. Particular groupings of plant species (specific plant communities) comprise the basis of different habitat types. In turn, animals help plants to reproduce through dispersal of pollen, fruits, or seeds. Consequently, plants and animals are interdependent, and certain plants and animals are often found together.

Some animals are migratory and are only present during certain times of year. Many animals' food needs change throughout the seasons or depending on their stage of growth. Climate changes threaten to uncouple many plant-animal relationships. For example, warmer winter temperatures may cause flowers to bloom before their migratory pollinators arrive in spring. Therefore, including a wide variety of food choices (native plants) in the landscape will provide for the changing needs of many animals.

Within a balanced landscape, native wildlife should not pose a nuisance or hazard to humans, and humans should be able to live in harmony with the wildlife. Some native animals, however, can be overabundant and may need to be discouraged in the landscape (e.g., deer, groundhogs, rabbits). A number of factors can cause native animals to become nuisance wildlife, particularly as a result of development pressures that alter habitat, food sources, or the presence of predators that normally keep populations in check. Feeding wildlife or leaving out garbage cans can attract animals such as squirrels, raccoons, deer, or bears, which may cause a nuisance situation in proximity to homes or other areas humans use.

In the Mid-Atlantic region, diseases transmitted by ticks to people and pets are a concern. In particular, deer ticks can transfer Lyme and other disease from mammals (mice, deer) to humans. To reduce the presence of ticks, use fencing to keep deer away from paths and buildings and reduce brushy areas near walkways and buildings. Strategic use of insect repellents, proper clothing, and routine body checks after being outdoors also help to reduce the risk of tick-borne disease. [For more information on ticks, see The Connecticut Agricultural Experiment Station *Tick Management Handbook*, Bulletin No. 1010, available online at **www.ct.gov/caes/**].

INVASIVE ANIMAL SPECIES

An invasive animal species is a species introduced outside of its native range that spreads rapidly (e.g. nutria, house sparrows, Asian tiger mosquitoes, emerald ash borers, Norway rats). Some invasive animals threaten native wildlife and plant populations and/or cause destruction of habitat areas, while others pose human health risks. [See Element 3, Invasive Plants, for links to invasive species lists]. As with plant species, identifying invasive animal species quickly can lead to much more successful control of the species. For well-established invasive animals, learn how to discourage their establishment and spread. For example, house sparrows will nest in bluebird boxes and kill nesting bluebirds. Houses can be designed to exclude house sparrows, or boxes can be monitored to evict nesting house sparrows. Always monitor new plantings for unknown insects and diseases, and avoid transporting firewood from distant places because it can harbor insects.

- Don't move firewood: **www.dontmovefirewood.org/**
- Center for Invasive Species and Ecosystem Health: **www.invasive.org/**
- Maryland Department of Agriculture mosquito control: **mda.maryland.gov/plants-pests/Pages/mosquito_control.aspx**

ECOSYSTEM

An ecosystem is a natural, interactive unit consisting of all plants, animals, and microorganisms in an area functioning together with all non-living physical factors of the environment. Living organisms are continually engaged in a set of relationships with every other element constituting the environment in which they exist. The interdependence of the life in an ecosystem heightens the importance of protecting all natural components, so that the thread that connects the web of life is not unraveled. [See Element 2, Native Plants].

WATER SOURCE

Water sources can be as large as a pond or as small as a dish of water on a balcony. Keep water sources clean and free of mosquito larvae.
- National Wildlife Federation (NWF): **www.nwf.org/How-to-Help/Garden-for-Wildlife/Gardening-Tips/Build-a-Backyard-Pond.aspx?campaignid=WH09ASLP&s_src=CWH_GoogleMini_ponds**
- U.S. Dept. of Agriculture, Natural Resources Conservation Service, Backyard Conservation program, backyard pond, wetland, and water feature information:
  www.nrcs.usda.gov/wps/portal/nrcs/detail/national/newsroom/features/?cid=nrcs143_023574

STRUCTURE

Instead of isolated plantings, such as a tree in the middle of lawn, group trees, shrubs and perennials to create layers of vegetation. A forest has, for example, a canopy layer (tallest trees), understory layers (various heights of trees and shrubs beneath the canopy) and a ground layer or forest floor. These layers provide the structure and variety needed for shelter, breeding or nesting space for a diversity of wildlife.

POLLINATORS

A diversity of insects act as pollinators in the Chesapeake Bay region. Honey bees are introduced pollinators, but native pollinators include solitary bees, wasps, flies, moths and butterflies. Different pollinators have different habitat requirements. The resources below provide information on pollinator habitat.
- North American Pollinator Protection Campaign **http://www.nappc.org** and
  http://www.nappc.org/pollinatorEn.html
- Xerces Society, conservation of butterflies and other invertebrates **http://www.xerces.org**

MORE RESOURCES

- Maryland Wild Acres program Invite Wildlife to Your Backyard...Some Tips for Creating a Wild Backyard: **www.dnr.state.md.us/wildlife/Habitat/WildAcres/**
- Virginia Department of Game and Inland Fisheries: **www.dgif.state.va.us/wildlifewatching/**
- District of Columbia Department of the Environment: **ddoe.dc.gov/service/fisheries-and-wildlife**
- Pennsylvania Department of Conservation and Natural Resources Wild Resources Conservation Program: **www.dcnr.state.pa.us/conserve/index.htm**
- West Viriginia Wild Yards Program: **www.wvdnr.gov/wildlife/wildyards.shtm**
- Audubon At Home **athome.audubon.org/** and Audubon Maryland-DC: **md.audubon.org/**
- Mizejewski, David. *Attracting Birds, Butterflies and Other Backyard Wildlife*. Creative Homeowner, 2004.
- Kress, Stephen W. *The Audubon Society Guide to Attracting Birds*. 2nd Edition. Cornell University, 2006.
- Tallamy, Douglas W. *Bringing Nature Home: How you Can Sustain Wildlife with Native Plants*. Updated and expanded. Timber Press, 2007. **www.timberpress.com/books/isbn.cfm/9780881928549**
- The Wild Ones Handbook (a "how to" to gardening for wildlife): **www.epa.gov/greenacres/wildones/**

5 HEALTHY AIR QUALITY

A conservation landscape promotes healthy air quality and minimizes air pollution.

An environmentally sound conservation landscape minimizes activities that directly create air pollution, promotes the use of trees and other plants that filter air pollutants, and eliminates or reduces the use of commercial products that are harmful or create polluting by-products.

Petroleum-fueled landscape tools produce pollutants responsible for poor air quality and create risks to human health and the environment. Through fuel combustion and evaporation processes, pollutants such as nitrogen oxides, sulfur dioxide, carbon dioxide, volatile organic compounds (VOCs), hydrocarbons, toxic chemicals, and particulate matter are released into the air. These pollutants contribute to the formation of ground-level ozone (also known as summertime smog) and regional haze, and to the deposition of nitrogen, acidic compounds, and mercury into sensitive ecosystems. Air pollutants that settle on land can then be carried by stormwater into local streams and rivers and affect water quality. The production and burning of fossil fuels also contributes to greenhouse gases that warm the atmosphere, creating long-term changes in climate.

The overuse or misapplication of commercial fertilizers and chemicals can directly and indirectly contribute to air pollution. For example, ammonia-based commercial fertilizers can release ammonia into the air. Ammonia can combine with other pollutants in the air and form fine particulate matter, which can impact human health and cause regional haze. Another example is the misapplication of pesticides, which can contaminate downwind areas and affect people and pets. Aerial spraying should be avoided on windy days.

HOW

There are many steps you can take to save energy through good planning and by selecting the right tools and plants.

- **Use adapted, non-invasive plants to reduce yard maintenance.** Site-appropriate plants will require less water, fertilizer, and chemicals, thereby reducing overall yard maintenance. This will reduce the need for gasoline-powered equipment such as lawn mowers, string trimmers, and leaf blowers. [See Element 2, Native Plants].

- **Landscape to improve energy conservation.** Plant additional native trees and shrubs near buildings for heating, cooling, and wind-protection benefits [See *Conserve Energy* in Element 8, Management]. This will reduce energy demands and will result in less air pollution. Further, the cooler air under shade trees reduces the rate of chemical reactions that produce precursors to smog.

- **Landscape to improve air filtration.** Plants clean outdoor air by filtering out particles or absorbing gases through their stomata and cuticles. Plants can store pollutants or break them down into other compounds. The degradation of carbon dioxide produces oxygen, which we need to breathe. Select native tree and plant species that are efficient in removing pollutants from the air, including species with leaf sizes and shapes that will capture gases, dust, and fine particles. Larger, broader leaves and those with fine hairs have more surface area to collect particles. The ability of a plant leaf to absorb gaseous atmospheric pollutants is determined by conductance of the stomata and is linked to the plant's genetics. There are varying degrees of resistance and susceptibility to pollution among plants. A good resource that provides information on tolerance of native species to urban conditions is *Native Trees, Shrubs, and Vines for Urban and Rural America: A Planting Design Manual for Environmental Designers* by **Gary L. Hightshoe** (1987, John Wiley & Sons).

  Trees are most efficient at cleaning the air. This is especially true for CO_2 emissions, as trees absorb CO_2 from the air, sequester (store) the carbon, and release oxygen into the air. One mature tree can remove 26 pounds of carbon dioxide from the atmosphere annually, the equivalent of 11,000 miles of car emissions [See **www.ext.vt.edu /pubs/envirohort/426-721/426-721.html**]. Many cities are looking into and employing "carbon offsets"—trying to counter the CO_2 produced as a result of human activities with the amount that tree plantings and forests can absorb. Using plants to clean the air and reduce the human-caused effects of air pollution is referred to as *phytoremediation*.

- **Decrease lawn area and reduce mowing time.** Create diverse habitats in your landscape by using native plants and trees and minimizing large expanses of lawn. This will reduce or eliminate the need to mow and spray. Small engines are big polluters. Less lawn means less time running a lawn mower. Plant and maintain your lawn according to the Cooperative Extension recommendations for your area. Use low-maintenance turf mixes that grow slowly and turf types that are adapted to your climate and the growing conditions in your yard.

  Operating a typical 4-horsepower gasoline powered lawnmower for 1 hour produces as much smog-forming hydrocarbons as driving an average car almost 200 miles under average conditions. Gasoline-powered string trimmers are actually *more polluting* than lawn mowers. [See **www.louisvilleky.gov/APCD/lawncare**.]

  A properly mown lawn is poor habitat for ticks, mosquitoes, and rodents. You can reduce the number of ticks immediately around your home by keeping grass mown and keeping tall grass and brushy areas away from buildings and walkways. [For further information, see **www.cdc.gov/ncidod/dvbid/lyme/index.htm**].

- **Use environmentally friendly yard equipment.** Replace old, polluting yard equipment with new, low or zero emission equipment. Recycle old equipment to prevent its continued use by others. Take it to a recycling center where it can be converted into raw material for use in cleaner equipment and other products. Ask your dealer about the new, cleaner gasoline equipment entering the market.

- **Maintain your equipment.** Change oil and clean or replace air filters regularly. Use the proper fuel/oil mixture in two stroke equipment. Tune up the engine, maintain sharp blades, and keep the underside of the mowing deck clean. Take time to winterize the equipment each fall.

- **Avoid spilling gasoline.** Even small gasoline spills evaporate and pollute the air. Use a gasoline container you can handle easily. Use a funnel and pour slowly and smoothly. If there is an ozone or unhealthy air advisory, do not fill or use gas-powered equipment. Keep the cap and vent hole on gasoline containers closed tightly. Transport and store gasoline-powered equipment out of direct sunlight and in a cool place. *Replace your old gas cans* with newer cans that have automatic shut-off, automatic closure, flow rate based on container capacity, and an anti-permeable lining that will control *VOC emissions*.

- **Consider cleaner options.** Electric equipment is cleaner than equipment powered by gasoline engines. Electric-powered lawn and garden tools produce essentially no pollution from exhaust emissions or through fuel evaporation. However, even electric power tools use energy that was, in many cases, produced by the burning of fossil fuels.

- **Use manual tools.** Tools that don't require electric or gasoline engines can be just as handy for small yards or small jobs. For smaller lawn areas, consider a reel mower, which produces no pollution and provides a good source of aerobic exercise. Rakes and brooms won't bite; and minimizing the use of blowers will reduce the amount of airborne dust and noise you generate. Reducing the need for yard maintenance equipment helps reduce sources of noise pollution. Trees and shrubs in the landscape also help to filter out noise pollution.

- **Minimize the use of toxic pesticide sprays.** Use integrated pest management (IPM) techniques to prevent and control infestations. Use homemade controls (such as soapy water sprays for aphids) or commercially available organic controls to control insect and disease outbreaks. [See *Manage Garden Pests with Integrated Pest Management (IPM)* in Element 8, Management.]

- **Little things add up.** Use and store yard chemicals and fertilizers appropriately to prevent evaporation or vaporization. Recycle or dispose of household and yard waste in an approved landfill rather than burning. Keep common allergen-producing plants such as ragweed off your property. Keep soil covered with mulch and plant material to reduce dust. Consider planting tree species with low *VOC emissions*.

LEARN MORE ABOUT IT

VOC EMISSIONS

Plants may release gases such as hydrogen sulfide that are considered to be air pollutants. If you live in an area where the air quality doesn't (or occasionally doesn't) meet established safety standards—often an issue in major metropolitan areas such as the Baltimore-Washington region—avoid planting trees that produce high amounts of "biogenic" (i.e., naturally produced) volatile organic compounds (VOCs). The ozone-forming potential of different tree species varies considerably—as much as 10,000 times. However, understand that the combined environmental benefits of trees far outweigh any adverse air quality impact from biogenic compounds, and thus planting trees is considered an important component of all urban environmental protection strategies. To aid in assessing the environmental impact of landscaped outdoor spaces, see the calculator at EcoSmart Landscapes, **www.ecosmartlandscapes.org/**.

6 CLEAN WATER

A conservation landscape conserves and cleans water.

Water is a precious and finite natural resource, an essential component in our lives and landscapes. Without it, nothing on Earth would survive. Less than 1 percent of all the water in the world is available as fresh clean water. Rainwater is constantly recycled through the ground and in the air, eventually becoming *groundwater* or *surface water*. Compacting soils and paving surfaces has decreased the likelihood that rainwater will enter the ground to complete the natural purifying cycle (Figure 1).

A conservation landscape preserves the natural water cycle and helps keep waterways clean in local watersheds. A *watershed* is all the land that drains after a rainfall to a particular body of water—a stream, river, pond, lake, or estuary such as Chesapeake Bay. Each watershed may be part of a larger watershed, as streams and rivers ultimately flow into larger water bodies such as the Bay. Rainwater running off the land carries with it chemicals, soil, plant debris, and other pollutants. Rainwater percolating into the land can also carry chemicals such as fertilizers, pesticides, and other toxins. Healthy soils and landscapes allow rainwater to penetrate the ground and help to filter out pollutants. Every piece of land has the ability to affect a waterway, whether it is above or below the ground. By using conservation landscaping techniques—and thus helping to reduce pollutants in the landscape, reduce wastewater amounts, increase groundwater recharge, and reduce water use—a landowner can help keep waterways clean *and* enjoy lower monthly water bills.

HOW

The amount of water used to maintain a lawn or garden can be reduced by as much as two-thirds during summer months by employing conservation landscaping practices that focus on these key elements: water zoning, plant selection, timing, thoroughness, proper equipment, mulching, and water retention and re-use.

- **Create water zones**. Arrange landscape, lawn, and garden areas in zones according to water need. (In arid parts of the country, this is called xeriscaping.) High water-use plants are grouped close to the water source (such as the hose connection); medium water-use plants and lawn areas can be farther from the water source; and low water-use plants, such as natives, can be sited on the perimeter of the property, or farthest from the water source. Designing the landscape and selecting plants to suit specific site conditions automatically reduces or eliminates the need to use this zoning plan, as all plants eventually require little or no watering. Keep in mind, however, that *every* plant needs some watering during the establishment period, so plan for access to a water source.

- **Select plants judiciously**. Choosing plants wisely is fundamental to reducing water use. When selecting plants for your landscape, choose those that are drought tolerant and adapted to your local weather conditions. Drought-tolerant species and those plants suited to existing soil moisture conditions will thrive once established with little or no supplemental watering. If the plant seems to require frequent watering, it's probably the wrong selection for that location. This is described fully in Element 2, Native Plants. Another example of conserving water through plant selection is to minimize the amount of lawn in the landscape. Lawns require more water, fertilizer, and gas-powered mowing equipment than does a planting of native plants.

- **Timing is key**. Water plants and lawns only when they need it. Water the lawn only when it exhibits signs of drought stress. A lawn will tell you when it needs watering; you have only to watch for the signs. When you walk across the grass and leave footprints that do not rapidly disappear, your lawn needs water. Water thoroughly to provide a good soaking. Drought-stressed shrubs or perennials will wilt. During severe drought, leaves may drop or turn yellow or brown and brittle. Well-established plants that were planted in appropriate conditions may occasionally wilt during the hottest part of the day. This is a natural defense to conserve water, and they should perk up as the sun shifts and the heat is reduced. If they remain wilted once the heat of the day has passed, they should be moved to a shadier, moister spot. Whether watering plants or lawn, water during the coolest part of the day to avoid unnecessary evaporation and wilting. Early morning is generally best, but early evening is acceptable on less humid days. Late evening watering can cause plants to stay wet all night, which encourages disease development. Watch the weather—there is no need to water if rainfall can do the job for you.

- **Give it a break**. During summer, *cool-season lawn grasses* such as fescues, bluegrass, and perennial rye naturally slow their growth as temperatures increase and rain decreases. Allow these grasses to go through their normal dormancy during hot summer months. Dormant lawn grass may turn brown. While this requires a change in aesthetic expectations, it will save significant water and normally will not harm the grass. The lawn will green up once autumn brings cooler weather and more rain.

- **Water thoroughly**. Water sufficiently and deeply, but not too often. Thorough watering promotes stronger root systems, enabling plants to find below-surface water during drought or hot weather. Watering too lightly or too often harms plants by encouraging shallow root systems, which make landscape plants more vulnerable to temperature extremes and the damage caused by drought and disease. Sufficient water should be delivered to the depth of the plants' roots, an *average* of 6 to 10 inches. The time it takes to deliver the proper amount of water to the soil depends on the watering method, equipment, soil type and moisture, and weather conditions at the time of watering. To determine an approximate delivery time, check the depth of soil moisture while watering and adjust for future applications based on prevailing conditions. When watering landscape plants, direct water to the base of the plant, not the leaves. Routinely watering the leaves wastes water through evaporation.

- **Use proper watering equipment**. Use equipment that delivers water efficiently to where it is specifically needed. For lawns and some landscaping areas, sprinklers or sprinkler systems will water deeply and appropriately if timing guidelines are followed and the mechanisms are aimed correctly at the target (though overhead watering loses water to evaporation and wind drift). Automatic systems should be set to detect moisture and bypass watering (or be turned off) if it rains. Soaker hoses can be used for shrubs and perennial beds to deliver deep watering over a few hours. Drip irrigation—which sends water straight to plants' roots with virtually no loss to evaporation—is the most efficient way to water shrubs, flower beds, vegetable gardens, and containers thoroughly and deeply.

- **Mulch properly**. Organic mulch retains soil moisture by reducing competition with weeds, shading the soil, and improving soil structure. This soil moisture can reduce the need for frequent watering of landscape plants. The depth of mulch needed is variable, depending on the type of soil and plants growing there. In general, mulch should not exceed a depth of 2 to 3 inches. Shallow-rooted plants such as azaleas should receive no more than an inch of pine-based mulch. Never place mulch in direct contact with the trunk or stem of trees and shrubs. Mulch should not be piled up around plants so water runs off instead of penetrating the soil. See *Ongoing Soil Maintenance in the Conservation Landscape* in Element 7, Soils, for more on mulch as it relates to soils.

- **Retain and reuse rainwater runoff**. Additional water conservation can be achieved through **stormwater management** practices. Reducing storm flow from a site prevents a surge of polluted runoff from entering local waterways. The following measures are some of the many ways that water can be slowed, retained, and used onsite:

  - Reduce *impervious surfaces*—reduce compaction in parking areas, driveways, and sidewalks by using alternative pavers that allow water to penetrate.

  - Encourage infiltration and avoid concentrating stormwater flows:

    - Replace a portion of lawn with landscaped areas;

    - Refrain from clearing trees and underbrush, especially on slopes, as the vegetation helps to slow runoff, and allows time for better absorption into the soil; plant native vegetation where stabilizing plants don't exist;

    - Create curved or meandering pathways on slopes instead of straight paths, as the latter makes a "raceway" for water and contributes to the slope's erosion;

    - Lengthen stormwater flow paths, providing long swales to carry rainwater from a site. Vegetation such as native bunch grasses in the swale helps to slow and filter runoff.

- Spread it out! Redirect runoff to multiple collection points onsite and distribute the water judiciously into the landscape
  - Install *rain gardens*, shallow depressions designed to retain rainwater for no longer than 24 hours, and planted with native plants that tolerate periodic flooding. These "bioretention" areas do not need to be large (compared to regular stormwater basins) and are as aesthetically appealing as "typical" landscaping beds. Rain gardens of any size are helpful. They provide a place to treat runoff onsite—pollutants settle out, sediment is trapped in the basin, and excess nutrients are used up by the plants—and slowly release cleaner water.
  - Direct downspouts, drains, sump discharges, and runoff from paved driveways, sidewalks, and patios into landscaped areas onsite. Do not direct runoff or any wastewater drainage offsite into a neighbor's property or public right of way.
  - Use a *rain barrel* to capture rainwater from downspouts and use it later for watering plants.
- **Plant a green roof to help absorb and use rainwater.** *Green roofs* are partially or completely covered with plants specifically suited to growing in shallow soil, full sun, and drought conditions. They benefit the environment by increasing surface area for collecting and using rainwater, removing nitrogen pollution in rain, neutralizing acid rain effect, and providing songbird habitat. They also reduce city "heat island" effect, carbon dioxide impact, summer air conditioning cost, winter heat demand, stormwater runoff, and noise.

LEARN MORE ABOUT IT

GROUNDWATER AND SURFACE WATER

Groundwater is water that percolates into the ground and exists beneath the earth's surface. It fills the pores between sand, clay, and rock and ultimately supplies wells and springs. Groundwater is a major source of water for agricultural and industrial purposes and is an important source of drinking water for about half of all Americans. *Groundwater recharge* is the replenishment of water that circulates in underground aquifers. Without recharge, we would not be able to draw water from wells or springs. Permeable surfaces are required to achieve groundwater recharge. *Infiltration* is the process of water penetrating the soil and percolating down through its structure (Figure 1)

Surface water is water located on the earth's surface in streams, ponds, wetlands, lakes, rivers, the Chesapeake Bay, and the ocean.

See **www.physicalgeography.net/fundamentals/8b.html for more information.**

WATERSHED

A watershed is all the land that drains after a rainfall to a particular body of water.
- **EPA** Surf your Watershed: **cfpub.epa.gov/surf/locate/index.cfm**
- Chesapeake Bay Foundation watershed information and action: **www.cbf.org**
- Chesapeake Bay Program, information, guidance, agreements, maps, etc.:
  www.chesapeakebay.net/discover/baywatershed

LAWN CARE/ WATERING

- Lawns and the Chesapeake Bay: **extension.umd.edu/sites/default/files/_docs/programs/bay-wise/FS702-LawnsAndChesapeakeBay.pdf**
- Lawn Reform Coalition: **lawnreform.org**
- Montgomery County, MD:
  www6.montgomerycountymd.gov/dectmpl.asp?url=/Content/dep/community/lawnGarden.asp
- University of Maryland Bay-Wise practices: **extension.umd.edu/baywise/home-landscape-best-management-practices**

COOL-SEASON LAWN GRASSES

Cool-season lawn grasses include Kentucky bluegrass, turf-type tall fescues, K-31 tall fescue, perennial rye grass, and fine fescues. Warm-season lawn grasses include Bermuda grass and buffalo grass. Cool-season grasses grow during cool weather beginning in fall whereas warm-season grasses green up in late-spring.

IMPERVIOUS SURFACES

Impervious surfaces are those surfaces in the landscape where rainfall cannot percolate into the ground, such as rooftops, pavement, sidewalks, driveways, parking lots, and compacted earth. Pervious or permeable surfaces are those areas with healthy, uncompacted soils, such as the forest floor, a meadow, a landscape bed, or a lawn that is not compacted.

Natural groundcover allows for greater infiltration and evapotranspiration, significantly reducing the amount of runoff leaving the site (as compared to sites with increased impervious surface) and contributing to groundwater recharge (Figure 1). AS LITTLE AS 10 PERCENT IMPERVIOUS COVER IN A WATERSHED CAN RESULT IN STREAM DEGRADATION.

Figure 1. Evapotranspiration rates decrease and runoff increases as impervious surface increases.

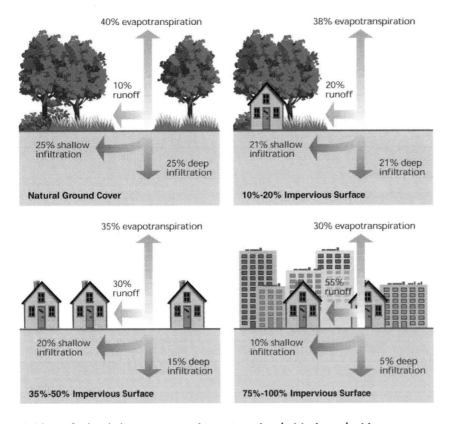

IMAGE SOURCE: IN STREAM CORRIDOR RESTORATION: PRINCIPLES, PROCESSES, AND PRACTICES (10/98), *BY THE FEDERAL INTERAGENCY STREAM RESTORATION WORKING GROUP (FISRWG)*

Guidance for local planners: **www.dnr.state.md.us/criticalarea/guidance.asp**

RAIN GARDENS AND RAIN BARRELS

Rain gardens are planted depressions in the land where runoff flows from impervious surfaces and is absorbed by the plants in the garden.

- Corinne Irwin's Conservation Landscaping: **mysite.verizon.net/irwinsothebay/**
- RainScapes: **www6.montgomerycountymd.gov/dectmpl.asp?url=/content/dep/water/rainscapes.asp**
- Chesapeake Ecology Center's Rain Gardens and Rainscaping initative: **www.ChesapeakeEcologyCenter.org**

Rain barrels are used to capture runoff from roofs: **www.rainbarrelguide.com**

GREEN ROOFS

Green roofs are a newer phenomenon in the United States but have been planted and maintained in Europe for years. They are not only aesthetically pleasing and environmentally beneficial, but they also can lengthen roof life by two to three times.

- Pennsylvania State University Green Roof Center: **plantscience.psu.edu/research/centers/green-roof**
- Green Roofs for Healthy Cities: **www.greenroofs.org/**
- Green roof industry: **www.greenroofs.com/**

7 HEALTHY SOILS

A conservation landscape promotes healthy soils.

Healthy plants begin with healthy soil. Soil contains a complex balance of minerals, water, air, and organic material (including living organisms). Soil supports plant roots and supplies nutrients, oxygen, and water. The structure and composition of the soil—the size and proportion of soil particles and the amount of organic material—affects how well the soil does these jobs. Large particles, such as sand, help soil drain quickly but do not store water or nutrients for plants. Small particles, such as clay and silt, hold nutrients and water well but drain poorly, and clay is hard to dig. Organic materials in the soil hold water, improve soil structure, nourish plants, and support the living organisms that keep the soil loose and fertile, and thus help plants fight pests and disease. Loamy soils that contain a balance of sand, silt, and clay and include organic matter are generally loose, well drained, and are able to store moisture and nutrients for plants. A loamy soil structure provides channels through which water and air can filter to greater depths. Air and water are, of course, essential; ideally they comprise about half of the volume of soil.

Soil composition varies considerably within a region and supports different plant and animal communities. Some soils are particularly unique and support unusual or rare plant and animal communities [See *Rare Soils*, below]. Native soils require thousands of years to evolve and can be destroyed in a moment. Disturbances can result in a breakdown of soil structure and create an imbalance of plant and animal communities. These disturbances may include compaction by heavy equipment or foot traffic, changes in nutrient cycling and pH from runoff and air deposition, removal of topsoil, erosion, and plowing. Thus, a cornerstone of conservation landscaping is the proper protection and ongoing care of the soil.

HOW

Soil Conservation Before and During Building Construction
Perhaps the greatest opportunities to protect native soils occur prior to and during building construction. Construction impacts soil in myriad ways. Natural soils are directly impacted as they are bulldozed, regraded, and paved over and topsoil can erode or become compacted or even be stripped from the site and sold. Conservation landscaping sensitivity during construction will protect the topsoil and native plant material through these important considerations:

- **Take measures to minimize grading damage.** Topsoil is a valuable resource, yet it is often damaged by grading during building construction. Design for minimum building and hardscape footprints and little or no grading. Make an explicit written agreement with grading contractors that topsoil is to remain onsite.

- **Store topsoil during construction.** Setting aside topsoil to be reapplied after construction is an option. Identify areas that will ultimately be paved as a place to store topsoil during construction. Store topsoil in piles no larger than six feet high to avoid suffocating the important soil organisms and to protect the piles from erosion. Topsoil stored during construction should be mixed with compost—one cubic yard of compost into 3–5 cubic yards of topsoil—before respreading.

- **Prevent compaction**. Air spaces in soil are important for plant health, soil organisms, and water infiltration, and activities that compress the air spaces out of soil must be avoided. Compaction causes damage that can take years or decades to recover, and it can be fatal to older trees at a construction site. Activities that cause soil compaction include grading, heavy equipment use during construction, heavy foot traffic, and parking.

- **Minimize the effect of vehicles and foot traffic during construction.** Before construction begins, designate parking areas away from trees and other planting areas. During construction, direct vehicle driving routes away from areas to be planted. Locate walkways in the most direct, convenient path so people don't create their own. Use plywood or a six-inch layer of bark mulch as a soil cushion (remove after work is completed). Avoid working with wet soil or during rain events.

- **Protect existing trees and their root zones during construction.** Install temporary fencing to keep construction activity from compacting the soil surrounding trees. At minimum, protect the area inside the dripline—the vertical line projected downward from the outermost edge of a tree's crown or canopy of the tree. Store equipment and materials elsewhere—areas that will be paved or built over are good sites for parking equipment. If spreading soil during construction, do not bury roots of existing trees and shrubs under more than 2 inches of added soil. Contact a certified arborist or tree specialist for onsite assistance.

- **Prevent erosion.** Soil washed from a site by erosion is a wasted resource. As it enters local water bodies, it carries pollutants, clouds the water, and can be damaging to aquatic resources. During construction, and to the fullest extent possible, cover bare ground with organic mulch or biodegradable geotextile fabric. Bare ground on steep slopes, near waterways, and soils that are easily eroded are of special concern. Replant these areas as soon as possible to help stabilize and reduce erosion of soil. A number of stabilization methods can be used while larger trees and shrubs become established: short-lived perennials such as black-eyed Susans or annual ryegrass can be used to fill in areas; any herbaceous plants can be installed, keeping in mind that they may become shaded out once trees mature. Applications of mulch may continue to be necessary to cover the soil until plants are well established.

Soil Care after Construction or in an Established Yard

Ultimately, your soil management program must respond to your existing site conditions. Conservation landscaping stresses working with existing conditions rather than trying to bend the site to suit desired plants. If you are fortunate, the topsoil wasn't stripped from your site or severely compacted during building construction. But some sites with extreme soil conditions may require altering in order to reestablish a healthy soil. Such conditions include compaction, low organic content, pH of less than 4.5 (highly acidic) or greater than 8.0 (very basic), sites where topsoil has been removed, etc. A basic soil test will provide critical information on soil composition, pH, and natural fertility. Amend soil only when existing conditions are severely limiting. If necessary, steps can be taken to reestablish a healthy soil.

- **If the soil is compacted, then it needs improvement.** As a basic test, poke a screwdriver into the soil. If you cannot achieve this without some effort, then the soil is compacted and requires some level of aeration. The easiest way to improve the soil is to add leaf mulch annually as a top dressing, and allow the natural processes of soil organisms to aerate the soil. Core aeration, rototilling, plowing, turning with shovels, or breaking the soil with a fork will reintroduce spaces for movement of water, oxygen, roots, and soil organisms. Choose first the least intrusive measure for aerating. For any method, organic matter will need to be added to improve the soil structure (see below). If improving the compacted condition is not possible, then raised planting beds are an alternative. Mechanical aeration such as tilling or double digging, if needed, should be done only in the year the planting bed is to be established—it does not need to be done annually, and, in fact, over tilling is detrimental to the soil. See separate guidelines for *farming or vegetable gardening soil improvements*, as these activities require more intervention than recommended for conservation landscaping.

- **Do not till if the soil is not compacted.** If you can slip a screwdriver easily into the soil, then it is not compacted and therefore does not need *tilling*. Although tilling can result in an immediate increase in air spaces, these cavities are not sustainable. Over the long term, tilling destroys soil structure and causes compaction. Tilling also accelerates the loss of soil organic material through decomposition. Soil organic material is critical to soil structure, soil organisms, and soil fertility. Tilling leaves the soil bare and susceptible to erosion, and brings weeds and other buried seeds to the surface where they will sprout. There are instances where tilling or another measure for aeration is appropriate, such as establishing a new planting bed.

- **Add organic matter where it is lacking.** In many landscapes, particularly around new construction, it may be necessary to add organic matter such as mature compost, composted manure, or leaf mold to rebuild soil structure. For soils that are extremely sandy, the organic material will help improve moisture retention and hold soil particles together better; for extremely clayey soils, it will help break up the clay and allow water and nutrients to move through the soil. The quantity and type to use depends on the existing soil and plans for landscaping. Consult with a local Cooperative Extension Service for recommendations.

- **Import soil as a last resort.** If there is little or no topsoil in which to plant for successful growth, consider bringing in soil from elsewhere. Keep in mind that you may be bringing in a source of undesirable weeds or invasive plants. Imported soil must be carefully selected to ensure good quality—this cannot be overstressed. Choose a reliable, knowledgeable source (for large site construction, the provider must certify that the soil is weed free). Inspect the soil before purchasing or accepting it. It should have good structure, friable (loose, crumbly) texture, an earthy smell, a brown (not gray or black) color, and it should be free of debris. Have the soil tested as you would test soil onsite, for its type or content (clay, loam, sand), pH, nutrients, organic matter, etc., and choose soil that best matches the subsoil at the site. The new soil should be lightly worked into the surface of the existing soil.

Ongoing Soil Maintenance in the Conservation Landscape

"Traditional" landscaping practices may base soil preparation on soil test results that describe how to change or amend the soil to make it appropriate for crop production (including ornamental plants). Conservation landscaping, by contrast, focuses on working with the existing soil conditions and choosing plants that will thrive in the site conditions with little or no intervention. Amendments are necessary where soil disturbances or extreme conditions severely limit native plant selection.

- **Choose native plants suited for the existing soil conditions.** Native plants have co-evolved with native soils and are adapted to grow in these soils without amendment. The best way to conserve a native soil is to keep it covered with native vegetation. A wide selection of native plants will thrive in sites with conditions most "traditional" gardeners would cringe at—hot, dry, sandy, acidic, nutrient-poor. Do not alter soil conditions to feature specific plants in a soil that otherwise would not support them. It is simpler and more sustainable and economical to simply use natives that are adapted to the ambient conditions. Exceptions, to some degree, must be made for turf areas and vegetable or cut flower gardens.

- **Change the pH only if absolutely necessary.** For conservation landscaping, a pH anywhere in the range of 4.5 to 8.0 can support a wide range of native plants. A _soil test_ will reveal the pH of your soil and guide your plant selection. If the soil test reveals a pH that is so extreme that it severely limits plant selection, then the soil can be altered by adding appropriate amounts of limestone to raise pH or elemental sulfur to lower it. Compost also helps ameliorate pH extremes. The soil test results will provide the appropriate recommendations for changing the pH, but this will likely not be necessary for most of your conservation landscape (only for extreme conditions). You may need to manage the pH in a vegetable garden, where the ideal pH for fertile soil is 6.5 to 7.0 (neutral). After applying amendments, it is important to test the soil again before finalizing the planting plan. Remember, the soil pH will not change overnight, and it may need testing and further amending in future years. Retest the soil every 3 to 5 years, and adjust accordingly.

- **Limit fertilization.** Conservation landscapes that use native plants suited to the existing site conditions are self-sustaining and do not benefit from fertilization. Small lawns and vegetable or cut flower gardens may require some fertilization, depending on the needs of the soil compared to the requirements of the plants to be grown. For these areas, test the soil to determine what nutrients are lacking and apply amendments accordingly. In some older neighborhoods, decades of lawn over-fertilization have caused phosphorus to build up in soils, making further applications unnecessary. In any case, applying excess fertilizer can be bad for plants and soil life, wastes money, and leads to water pollution. Too much fertilizer results in weak and tender plants that are especially appetizing to pests. Nitrogen that cannot be used by the plants leaches into groundwater or runoff, and excess phosphorus can be carried away with eroding soils. It is also important to fertilize at the appropriate time. For example, fertilizing cool-season grasses in spring can actually help weeds outcompete the grass. Retest the soil every 3 to 5 years, and adjust accordingly. For more information on _proper timing and amounts of fertilization_, see University of Maryland Extension's Home and Garden Information Center, **www.extension.umd.edu/hgic**.

- **Conservation landscapes recycle organic materials onsite.** Whenever possible, use organic material from the site itself, such as fallen leaves and needles from trees onsite. This debris is part of the natural process of decomposition that is important to the soil and the needs of those trees. If mulch must be brought in, purchase from a reputable or known source to be sure of the quality of material. Some mulches, particularly those that are dyed (red, black, or other colors), contain shredded material from old wooden pallets, discarded furniture, demolished buildings, or lumber scraps. These are not appropriate quality to use with plants because they may contain toxins, nails, and other debris. Mulch applied for weed prevention needs to be free of weed seed, an occasional problem with free mulches such as those obtained from community leaf collection or composting programs. Do not use peat moss, as it is mined from living bogs and is not a renewable resource.

- **Use mulch judiciously.** The use of mulch can be desirable in landscaping beds and vegetable gardens to help prevent weed growth, retain soil moisture, and encourage soil structure to develop over time. Soil surfaces should be covered with mulch, organic debris, or a dense cover of plants at all times to prevent erosion and control weed growth. However, excessive use of organic matter is discouraged because it contains nutrients and organic compounds that will become part of the site runoff and contribute to water pollution. Symptoms in plants of excess organic material include unusual height, breadth, and falling over. Some native plants require less fertile soil conditions, and compost may not be necessary. Soil that is too rich also promotes weed growth.

- **Determine the appropriate <u>type</u> of mulch to use.** The type of mulch used needs to be appropriate to the requirements of the plants in the landscape. Acidic mulch, such as pine needles or bark, is appropriate for plants that prefer acidic soils but will damage plants that require more basic conditions. Hardwood bark mulch (pH 7.0-8.0) may be used for newly installed landscaping or plants that require basic conditions, but should be applied to a depth of only one inch so it will remain drier and therefore will not decompose quickly. For annual (or as needed) mulching, larger particle size mulches (wood chips or bark nuggets) will last longer in your landscape but may be more susceptible to washout. Smaller particle size mulches (shredded bark/wood/leaves or pine needles) will be more resistant to washout. Wood chips or bark can be excellent choices for lining garden paths and will promote beneficial fungi and microorganisms that help nourish native woodland plants.

- **Determine the appropriate <u>amount</u> of mulch to use.** To figure out how much organic material a plant species needs, take a look at the plant's natural habitat. Native plants that thrive best in rich, organic soils require more mulch. Many woodland and wetland species appreciate organic matter, whereas plants native to dunes, steep slopes, and dry meadows do best in lean (nutrient-poor) soils and thus require less mulch. In any case, the depth of mulch around plants should not exceed 2 to 3 inches, and it should be cleared from direct contact with plant stems, trunks, or bark. See the table below for a formula to calculate the amount of mulch needed for a given area.

LEARN MORE ABOUT IT

RARE SOILS

Some soils are unique and should be given great consideration when planning construction or landscaping activities at a site. Examples of unusual soils in the Chesapeake watershed include organic soils (outside of the tidal zone), soils developed over ancient shell middens, and soils over unique bedrock (such as thin soils over serpentine bedrock). Unique soils are often associated with unusual plant and animal communities. For assistance in identifying soils and appropriate conservation strategies, consult with natural resource experts such as state or federal soil scientists, wetland delineators, foresters, and botanists. Good contacts include the Natural Resource Conservation Service or your local Agricultural Extension Agent.

SOIL AMENDMENTS FOR FARMING OR VEGETABLE GARDENING

See University of Maryland Extension publications links (Soil Fertility/ Irrigation and other factsheets): **pubs.agnr.umd.edu/Category.cfm?ID=L#subCat24** and other state extension publications.

TILLING

See also links above to general soils information.
- Owen, Marion. "Roto-tilling is a No-No": **www.plantea.com/no-tilling.htm**

SOIL TESTING LABS

- Maryland: **www.hgic.umd.edu/_media/documents/hg110a_007.pdf**
- Pennsylvania: **www.aasl.psu.edu/ssft.htm**
- Virginia: **www.soiltest.vt.edu/**
- West Virginia: **plantandsoil.wvu.edu/research_areas/soil_testing_lab**

REFERENCES AND RESOURCES

- Building Healthy Soil: **pubs.ext.vt.edu/426/426-711/426-711.html**
- Saving Your Soil and the Chesapeake Bay: **extension.umd.edu/learn/saving-your-soil-and-chesapeake-bay**
- Soils for Salmon (guidance from Washington State for homeowners and others to protect water quality): **www.soilsforsalmon.org/how.htm#homeowners**
- Nutrient Management In Your Backyard: **www.nrcs.usda.gov/wps/portal/nrcs/detail/national/newsroom/features/?cid=nrcs143_023538**
- Lowenfels, J. and W. Lewis. *Teaming with Microbes: The Organic Gardener's Guide to the Soil Food Web.* Timber Press 2010.
- Symphony of the Soil Project (Films about healthy soils and sustainable soil practices) http://www.symphonyofthesoil.com/

To calculate **AMOUNT OF MULCH NEEDED**
(or amount of topsoil for filling an undesirable depression or creating a raised bed)

The volume is measured in cubic yards (CY) = # cubic feet ÷ 27
Cubic feet (ft^3) = square feet (*) x feet (ft) [* square feet: Sq Ft, SF, or ft^2]

Formula:
$$\frac{\text{Planting Area (SF) x (Depth in feet)}}{27} = \text{\# CY}$$

Depth for mulch is a matter of inches, but it needs to be converted to feet for the calculation:
1 inch deep = 1 ÷ 12 = .083 ft.
2 inches deep = 2 ÷ 12 = .16 ft.
3 inches deep = 3 ÷ 12 = .25 ft.

To calculate **soil volume for a raised mound**, use the desired height:
8 inches high = 8 ÷ 12 = .67 ft. … and so on.

If not using bulk mulch, then determine the appropriate number of bags of mulch needed:
1 CY = 9 bags mulch or soil if each bag holds 3 cu ft. = 13.5 bags if bags hold 2 cu ft. each

8 MANAGEMENT

A conservation landscape is managed to conserve energy, reduce waste, and eliminate or minimize the use of pesticides and fertilizers.

How we all live on the land is important, so how each of us manages our property is important to all of us. How you manage your own or your client's landscape can have an important impact on the health of your local environment and the Chesapeake Bay. Embrace that responsibility; be a guardian of the property. Your landscape may be the one piece of land you have full opportunity to manage well.

The rewards of a well-maintained conservation landscape are many. It reflects positively on its owner and the professional who maintains it. It beautifies the home and neighborhood. It affords a comfortable place to entertain and offers a place for relaxation. Most importantly, it provides and promotes a safe environment for the property owner to use and enjoy.

Nothing worth having comes for free, and no conservation landscape happens without some work. But conservation landscaping doesn't have to require more time than a conventional landscape. Setting up an endless cycle of continual human intervention wastes both time and resources. Furthermore, intensive maintenance practices such as overuse of chemical pesticides and herbicides, excessive or poorly timed watering, and frequent mowing and trimming tend to be environmentally damaging. To reduce the need for intensive maintenance, develop a site management program that works with natural processes, recycles resources onsite, and achieves a self-sustaining landscape.

HOW

Reduce Your Waste Stream

Prevent fertilizer, pesticides, yard debris, and pet waste from entering the waste stream or becoming pollution in local waterways. Reduce, reuse, and recycle are watchwords in conservation landscaping. Reducing waste starts with not generating it in the first place.

- **Select the right plant for the right place.** Plants suited to the site conditions will thrive and are less susceptible to disease and pests. Carefully chosen plants, placed where they can grow to their natural size and shape, are healthier and more attractive.

- **Prune selectively to complement the natural form and strengthen the structure of your plants.** Selective pruning avoids unnecessary plant debris. Watering and fertilizing wisely prevents rampant plant growth that weakens the plants and generates plant waste. In particular, don't overwater or over-fertilize lawn, as these practices create the need to mow more frequently.

- **Practice grasscycling.** When mowing lawn, cut the grass at the highest setting and allow the clippings to filter down into the turf as a natural fertilizer.

- **Compost plant and grass trimmings, leaves, and other organic material.** Using the compost as mulch or natural fertilizer improves soil structure and fertility. Build a compost pile or participate in local yard waste collection programs to keep plant material out of local landfills. Dumping yard waste offsite is discouraged!

- **Get creative in your material use.** Material use is another important consideration in conservation landscaping. Using recycled content and salvaged, durable, or local materials conserves resources and reduces the amount of embodied energy that is consumed by the landscape.

- **Water wisely.** Overwatering wastes resources, is not good for the lawn or the garden, and spreads pollutants to other sites and to waterways as wastewater leaves the site.

Manage Garden Pests with Integrated Pest Management (IPM)

The ability to identify specific pest or disease problems and treat them effectively is key to maintaining a healthy landscape. Pesticides, herbicides, and fungicides are toxic and can pollute groundwater and nearby waterways, and harm wildlife, pets, and family members. To keep your landscape safe and healthy for your family's enjoyment, practice integrated pest management. IPM offers an ecological approach to controlling pests and disease. For more information on IPM, see the links at the end of this section.

- **Monitor regularly for signs of plant problems and insect pests.** Apply controls before pest or disease problems get out of hand. Obviously it is critical to know the pest and its life cycle; contact your local Cooperative Extension for help identifying the pest before choosing a control method.

- **Pesticides should not be used routinely or indiscriminately.** It is unrealistic to expect a totally pest- and disease-free landscape. IPM advocates the tolerance of occasional minor pest outbreaks wherever possible. Recognize that some plant damage is okay and will likely not affect the long-term health of the plant. In fact, allowing a low level of pest presence will attract beneficial insects and songbirds that will aid in controlling the pests.

- **When control is necessary, use the least toxic methods of pest control first.** Hand picking insect pests and diseased leaves from plants will often be sufficient. Removing weeds when they are young and tender requires less effort. Insect traps and weed barriers are non-toxic control options. When necessary, use environmentally friendly and/or organic pesticides such as horticultural oils and soaps, *Bacillus thuringiensis* (Bt), and botanical insecticides whenever possible. Other pest prevention ideas include removing plant debris and diseased plants to prevent the spread of disease from one season to the next; choosing resistant varieties of plants, especially local native plants; and using plants (such as members of the mint and aster families) that attract beneficial insects to the garden.

- **Use pesticides ONLY when and where they are absolutely needed and only as instructed on the label.** Before using pesticides or fertilizers, read and follow the label. The label is the law. Dispose of unused pesticides and fertilizers through local hazardous waste recycling programs. By all means, keep pets and children away from areas treated with pesticides. Remember, it is poison!

Control Undesirable Vegetation

A "weed" can be any plant that is out of place, growing where it doesn't "belong," ecologically speaking, or where it is not wanted in landscaping. Some tolerance for weeds helps to reduce the tendency to overmanage the landscape. Furthermore, the prevalent human preference for "tidiness" in the landscape is contributing to a reduction in our regional biodiversity. Developing an understanding of plant values and allowing some areas to remain "naturalized" as appropriate will help to remove the stress on natural resources. Many native species that some people consider "weeds" are important to the survival of insects and other wildlife.

However, there are certainly situations where vegetation removal or control is necessary. Unwanted plants that volunteer in a planting bed and outcompete what was planted, or detract from desired aesthetics, will need to be removed. Aggressive and invasive plants (especially state-designated "noxious" weeds) will require control. When removing vegetation, choose the method that will have the least negative effects on the soil, plants, animals, local water or air quality, and people. (For more information on these measures, see Element 7, Healthy Soils, and Element 3, Invasive Plant Management.)

- **Manual plant removal.**
  - Pulling is advisable for small, manageable situations. Be sure to remove as much of the roots as possible. Gloves and protective clothing help prevent skin rash, irritation, or injury from many types of plants.

  - Smothering or solarizing plants and seeds with materials such as layers of paper, heavy mulch, fabric, or black plastic is an environmentally sound option that requires time—possibly several weeks. Solarizing must be done in the heat of summer and requires soil moisture for success. Dead vegetation will need to be removed by raking or allowed to decompose fully into the soil. Solarizing will not effectively control plants with aggressive root systems.

- **Mechanical plant removal.**

  - Use hand tools such as shovels, cultivators, hoes, and weed-pulling devices to remove entire plants. Propane torches or steam may be used for spot-treating individual plants or small areas. Fire protection measures and permits are necessary for flame use. Burning is not suitable for poison ivy as it spreads toxic fumes.

  - Use machinery to mow or cut vegetation to prevent seeding and vegetative spread, such as by rhizomes or vines. For some plants, cutting only multiplies their sprouting, so proper plant identification and control information are important to successful removal. Some woody plants can be removed with one cutting. Other plants, particularly herbaceous species, will require repeated cutting and may need complete removal by another means.

  - Shallow tilling, while not promoted because of its ability to destroy soil structure and contribute to compaction, may be prescribed to eradicate weed seeds present in the soil, particularly to prepare a site for lawn or meadow seeding. A program of repeated tilling, or alternate tilling and herbiciding, may be needed. Shallow tilling means a maximum depth of one to two inches. Remember that tilling is a disturbance that brings weeds to the surface where they will grow, so it can increase the weed problem if not done repeatedly to fully eradicate weeds.

- **Chemical control.** In an IPM program, chemical measures may be a last resort, and organic alternatives such as corn gluten products or natural acetic acids are encouraged when appropriate. For large areas impacted by invasive species, the application of herbicides is often less harmful than the long-term negative effects of the invasive plants.

  Do your homework before using any chemical. Check the manufacturer's website for specific information on contents, safety, and use; consider side effects to non-target plant species, children, adults with chemical sensitivity, pets, and wildlife including insects and aquatic life; determine the chemical's effectiveness and specificity for the plant(s) to be controlled, application method and timing of application, and its breakdown time or persistence in the soil. For specific advice, it is best to consult a weed specialist through the state or local agriculture department.

- **General considerations**. Minimize soil disturbance, as it invites more weeds. Prevent further spread by cleaning seeds and root material from clothing and equipment prior to moving to another site. Do not compost weeds or chemically treated vegetation. Bag invasives and dispose in a landfill so they will not resprout or spread seeds.

Conserve Energy

With the use of mowers, blowers, weed whips and saws, chemical fertilizers, and pesticides, conventional landscape maintenance is very consumptive of fossil fuels. The need to conserve energy is as important in conservation landscaping as the need to conserve water.

- **Well placed trees can reduce energy use in buildings.** When properly placed, mature trees can reduce the interior temperature of a building by as much as 20 degrees, reducing summer cooling costs by 25–40 percent. Select and place trees to shade adjacent buildings in the summer or protect them from prevailing winter winds. It's also helpful to shade your air conditioner and paved areas. Plant trees to the west and southwest of a building for maximum shading benefit. Avoid planting trees that block solar collectors or in front of south-facing windows that allow the low winter sun to warm a home. Large deciduous trees will be of greater value for summer cooling and winter solar gain. Select native evergreen trees for windbreaks, and plant them on the north and west sides of your property where they will shield your home from chilling winter winds.

- **Reduce the amount of lawn in your landscape.** Lawn mowing is easily the most energy consumptive routine landscape maintenance practice. The unavoidable fact is that reducing the amount of lawn in the landscape is an important step toward reducing energy consumption. Keep enough lawn for specific recreational or aesthetic needs, and convert the rest to more environmentally friendly plantings. Lawns also provide relatively little habitat or food value for wildlife.

- **Choose and maintain your garden equipment with energy conservation in mind.** When using machinery, choose the smallest, most fuel efficient, lowest emission machinery required to get the job done. Use hand-powered equipment whenever possible. Electric garden tools using energy produced in regulated power plants is inherently less polluting than small gas-powered equipment. While they tend to be less powerful, they are more than adequate to the task for most small landscape settings.

- **Use recycled materials, and avoid petroleum-based products, including synthetic fertilizers.** Remember, recycling plant debris on site will minimize fuel consumption for creating manmade products. What's more, buying local products reduces the hidden environmental costs of transporting materials, such as pollution and energy consumption.

<u>Tell the Neighbors and Your Clients about It</u>
Neighbors will be curious about conservation landscaping activities, especially as a yard takes on some new characteristics. Their curiosity is an opportunity. Tell them about it. You can help educate them about your process of creating a conservation landscape. Ideally, the conservation landscape will become an example that encourages other members of the community to follow suit, and conservation landscapes are even more effective when they occur in groups or corridors. The more people that know about conservation landscaping, the better. There is strength in numbers. Spread the word!

→ Check out one community example—*Naturescaping: Appreciating, Preserving and Restoring Reston's Natural Resources*, Reston Association (Virginia), and more publications:
https://www.reston.org/ParksRecreationEvents/Nature/Publications/Default.aspx?qenc=HzT9ACzZbNs%3d&fqenc=j1xqX3FCgDvWnUYCHXVUsw%3d%3d

LEARN MORE ABOUT IT

A Few of Many Resources for Garden and Landscape Management and Care
- Pruning Ornamental Plants:
  http://extension.umd.edu/sites/default/files/_images/programs/hgic/Publications/HG84_Pruning%20ornamental%20plants.pdf
- Pruning Ornamental Trees and Shrubs:
  http://extension.umd.edu/sites/default/files/_images/programs/hgic/Publications/non_HGIC_FS/EB150.pdf
- Lawns and the Chesapeake Bay: **extension.umd.edu/publications/PDFs/FS702.pdf**
- How to Choose a Lawn Care Service That's Right for You...and the Chesapeake Bay:
  www.hgic.umd.edu/_media/documents/HowtoChooseaLawnCareServiceMDA15.06.06_000.pdf
- Landscapes that help the Chesapeake Bay: **extension.umd.edu/publications/PDFs/FS701.pdf**
- University of Maryland Extension Home and Garden Information Center (HGIC) factsheets and more:
  http://extension.umd.edu/hgic/information-library/home-and-garden-information-center-publications
- Integrated Pest Management
  - HGIC: and click on the IPM link;
  - National IPM Center: **northeastipm.org/whatis.cfm**;
  - U.S. Environmental Protection Agency IPM principles: **www.epa.gov/pesticides/factsheets/ipm.htm**.

A Few of Many Conservation Landscaping Programs including links to references, nurseries, and more
- Audubon at Home, National Audubon Society and Audubon Maryland-DC: **www.audubonathome.org**
- Backyard Conservation, USDA Natural Resources Conservation Service:
  www.nrcs.usda.gov/wps/portal/nrcs/detail/national/newsroom/features/?cid=nrcs143_023574
- BayScapes Program, The Alliance for Chesapeake Bay: **www.allianceforthebay.org**
- BayScapes Program, U.S. Fish and Wildlife Service: **www.fws.gov/chesapeakebay/Bayscapes.htm**
- Bay-Wise Program, Maryland: **www.extension.umd.edu/baywise**
- Chesapeake Conservation Landscaping Council: **www.chesapeakelandscape.org**
- Ecological Landscaping Association: **www.ecolandscaping.org/**
- MidAtlantic Ecological Landscapes Partnership (MAEscapes): **extension.psu.edu/plants/gardening/maescapes**

SEASONAL MAINTENANCE: A Sample Conservation Landscaping Calendar

Maintenance such as pruning requires knowledge of specific plant species and their habits and requirements, while some maintenance practices are more generally applied. In conservation landscaping, some "traditional" practices may be left out altogether. If you are used to regularly scheduled cutting, shearing, clearing, fertilizing, and so on, you will find this approach very different. The schedule described here is only an example, taken from a model conservation landscaping project. A customized schedule could be developed for each site as a new service to offer customers, or you may find some common practices here to promote and use more widely.

LATE FALL/WINTER (late October/early November):
Leave most plants standing throughout winter, as long as is aesthetically possible, to provide cover and food/seed for birds and overwintering insects.
- remove dead canes that have fallen over; leave all remaining plants standing;
- dig fresh edges of garden beds (trenches) as necessary;
- manually remove remaining weeds and stray turfgrass such as crabgrass;
- mulch bare areas 1 to 2 inches deep with an appropriate organic mulch to improve appearance, help prevent late season weeds, and provide winter protection;
- identify problem areas from the growing season and plan management strategies before the spring season (for example, recurring weeds that will need early spring direct application of a specific, safe pre-emergent herbicide);
- divide/ remove plants that have spread as necessary/as appropriate, depending on species (divide some species in spring);
- remove and dispose of plant parts that are harboring pests, such as overwintering borers, or disease that could spread, such as fungus (do not compost these materials).

WINTER (November through February):
- monthly, check for any areas needing early removal of spent vegetation for aesthetic reasons—such as after a particularly heavy snowfall (after snow melts);
- confirm and/or adjust management plans for upcoming year;
- prune shrubs and trees minimally as necessary and as appropriate to particular species, using naturalistic/ selective pruning (as opposed to shearing and shaping), some multi-stemmed trees are <u>desired</u>.

LATE WINTER/EARLY SPRING (mid- to late March):
- cut back all perennial plants and remove cut vegetation—bunch grasses should be cut back to a height of 4-6 inches; leave all green basal leaves of plants (such as black-eyed Susans);
- rake area <u>lightly</u> (thorough cleanup is not necessary; some organic debris such as light leaf litter is desired and necessary for plant and animal health, though diseased plant material may be clipped and disposed of;
- add 1 to 2 inches of an appropriate organic mulch to all bare, open areas of garden beds, being careful not to bury seedlings or new growth of emerging perennials (do <u>not</u> create mulch "volcanoes" around trees or pile mulch up against tree trunks/bark)—if mulch was applied in the fall, this may not be needed, do not re-mulch if a healthy layer exists;
- dig new trench edge to garden beds;
- if adjacent turf areas or paths require spot overseeding, avoid spreading seed in garden areas.

SPRING/SUMMER (April-September):
- weed (manually) once per month (twice monthly may be necessary April through June) to remove commonly recognized weeds—identification is important for allowing the native species planted in the garden to spread as desired;
- divide/remove plants that have spread as necessary/ as appropriate depending on species (divide some species in fall);
- mow grass paths or edges as needed;
- maintain garden edge as needed;
- water ONLY during extended periods of drought, as plants begin to show signs of stress—many native plant species tolerate normal periods of hot, dry weather; a few will not survive over-watering;
- trim asters, removing up to a third of the plant's height every 2 weeks mid-May to July 1 to promote branching so plants will support a heavy bloom;
- lawn treatment (if any) should be part of an approved IPM program, and only prescribed where lawn health and annual soil tests deem necessary.

Made in the USA
Coppell, TX
06 November 2020